Pebble®
Plus

Cool Sports Facts

# Cool Football Facts

by Kathryn Clay

Consulting Editor: Gail Saunders-Smith, PhD

Consultant: Craig Coenen, PhD
Associate Professor of History
Mercer County Community College
West Windsor, New Jersey

CAPSTONE PRESS
a capstone imprint

Pebble Plus is published by Capstone Press,
151 Good Counsel Drive, P.O. Box 669, Mankato, Minnesota 56002.
www.capstonepub.com

Books published by Capstone Press are manufactured with paper
containing at least 10 percent post-consumer waste.

*Library of Congress Cataloging-in-Publication Data*
Clay, Kathryn.
  Cool football facts / by Kathryn Clay.
    p. cm.—(Pebble plus. Cool sports facts)
  Includes bibliographical references and index.
  Summary: "Simple text and full-color photos illustrate facts about the rules, equipment, and records of football"—
Provided by publisher.
  ISBN 978-1-4296-4476-1 (library binding)
  ISBN 978-1-4296-7384-6 (paperback)
  1. Football—Miscellanea—Juvenile literature.  I. Title. II. Series.

GV950.7.C59 2011
796.332—dc22                                                        2009051410

**Editorial Credits**
Erika L. Shores, editor; Kyle Grenz, designer; Eric Gohl, media researcher; Eric Manske, production specialist

**Photo Credits**
AP Images/LM Otero, 21
Corbis/Bettmann, 19; Reuters/Tim Shaffer, 13
Dreamstime/Ken Durden, cover; Wisconsinart, 15
Getty Images Inc./George Gojkovich, 9; George Rose, 5; Michael Burr, 7; Nick Laham, 17
Landov LLC/Boston Globe/John Bohn, 11
Shutterstock/Trinacria Photo, cover (football), back cover, 1

## Note to Parents and Teachers

The Cool Sports Facts series supports national social studies standards related to people, places,
and culture. This book describes and illustrates football. The images support early readers
in understanding the text. The repetition of words and phrases helps early readers learn new
words. This book also introduces early readers to subject-specific vocabulary words, which are
defined in the Glossary section. Early readers may need assistance to read some words and to
use the Table of Contents, Glossary, Read More, Internet Sites, and Index sections of the book.

Printed in the United States of America in North Mankato, Minnesota.
072011       006231CGVMI

# Table of Contents

# Touchdown!

More than 90 million people watch the NFL Super Bowl on TV each year. In 1990, the San Francisco 49ers amazed fans with a record 55 points.

NFL stands for National Football League.

# Cool Equipment

Teams that play outside have 48 footballs ready for each game. Games played indoors use only 36 footballs.

Quarterbacks started wearing radio headset helmets in 1994. Coaches talk to the quarterback from the sidelines.

# Cool Rules

Players can't celebrate too much after a touchdown. In 2008, Wes Welker paid a $10,000 fine for making a snow angel.

Players can't rough the punter or kicker. Breaking the rule is a 15-yard penalty.

# Cool Records

In 1894, deaf quarterback Paul Hubbard first used the huddle. He didn't want other teams to see his signs.

As a starting quarterback,

Brett Favre has beaten

every team in the NFL.

He is the only player

to hold this record.

Kicker Tom Dempsey had
no toes on his right foot.
That didn't stop him from
kicking a 63-yard field goal.

Deion Sanders played in both the NFL's Super Bowl and Major League Baseball's World Series. No other athlete holds this record.

# Glossary

**deaf**—being unable to hear

**huddle**—a group of football players planning the next move

**penalty**—a punishment for breaking the rules

**rough**—to tackle and knock down

**sideline**—the line that marks the edge of a football field

**Super Bowl**—the championship game of the National Football League

**touchdown**—a six-point score in a football game

# Read More

**Gigliotti, Jim**. *Football*. Innovation in Sports. Ann Arbor, Mich.: Cherry Lake, 2009.

**Kalman, Bobbie, and John Crossingham**. *Huddle Up Football*. Sports Starters. New York: Crabtree, 2007.

# Internet Sites

FactHound offers a safe, fun way to find Internet sites related to this book. All of the sites on FactHound have been researched by our staff.

Here's all you do:

Visit *www.facthound.com*

FactHound will fetch the best sites for you!

# Index

Word Count: 178

Grade: 1

Early-Intervention Level: 21